In my family,
we celebrate with lights.
Can you guess what
we call our celebration?

My family celebrates Hanukkah.
We light the menorah for eight nights.

In my family,
we celebrate with lights.
Can you guess what
we call our celebration?

My family celebrates Christmas.
We decorate our tree with lights.

In my family,
we celebrate with lights.
Can you guess what
we call our celebration?

My family celebrates Kwanzaa.
We light the kinara for seven nights.

In my family,
we celebrate with lights.
Can you guess what
we call our celebration?

My family celebrates
Chinese New Year.
We light lanterns.

What other celebrations use lights?